NEW FOREST RECIPES

compiled by
Dorothy Baldock

with illustrations by
Wilfred Ball RE
and **Walter Tynedale**

SALMON

Index

- Bachelor's Pudding 26
- Bean and Bacon Soup 10
- Buttered Trout 31
- Cornflour Cake 38
- Cucumber and Stilton Mousse 35
- Devilled Chicken 34
- Farmhouse Halibut 16
- Gypsy Bread 13
- Hampshire Cod 7
- Hampshire Drops 44
- Hampshire Goose 20
- Hampshire Haslet 37
- Hampshire Herrings 41
- Hampshire Roll 47
- Hampshire Syllabub 43
- Honey and Walnut Tartlets 11
- Lardy Cake 28
- Lenten Pie 19
- Mothering Sunday Wafers 8
- Mustard Rabbit 17
- New Forest Venison 25
- Picnic Cake 22
- Poacher's Pie 40
- Pork with Nuts 32
- Strawberries in Syrup 14
- Syrup Roll 5
- Venison Casserole 4
- Venison Pasty 46
- Watercress Flan 23

Cover pictures: *front:* A cottage near Ringwood *back:* Swan Green, Lyndhurst
title page: Rufus Stone *facing page:* Queen's Bower

Printed and Published by Dorrigo, Manchester, England. © Copyright.
All rights reserved. No part of this publication may be reproduced, stored in a retrieval system or transmitted, in any form or by means, electronic, mechanical, photocopying or otherwise. Images/Recipes J Salmon Ltd

Venison Casserole

2 lb. venison, wiped and cut into cubes
2 oz. flour
Salt and black pepper
Pinch of dry mustard
2 oz. lard or 2 tablespoons olive oil and ½ oz. butter
2 large onions, peeled and chopped
2 sprigs thyme
¾ pint stock
¼ pint port wine
6 oz. mushrooms, wiped and sliced
1 lb. potatoes, peeled and left whole
1 oz. butter, melted

Set oven to 300°F or Mark 2. Mix the flour, seasoning and mustard and coat the venison. Heat the lard or the oil/butter in a pan and brown the meat on all sides. Transfer to a casserole. Fry the onion in remaining fat, transfer to casserole and add the thyme. Pour stock into the pan and bring to the boil, stirring. Pour over the meat and onions. Cover and cook for ¾ hour. Remove from the oven, add the port wine and mushrooms and cook for further 30 minutes. Meanwhile, boil potatoes until just soft, but not crumbly. Cool a little, then slice. Remove casserole from oven and arrange sliced potatoes on the top in slightly overlapping layers, brush with melted butter and return to oven, without the lid, for further 30 minutes or until potatoes are golden. Traditionally served with boiled leeks and mashed swede. Serves 4 to 6.

Syrup Roll

8 oz. prepared suet pastry
4 oz. golden syrup
1 teaspoon ground ginger or
the grated rind of a lemon

Roll out the suet pastry on a lightly floured surface to form a strip 8-10 inches long. Spread the syrup to within 1 inch of the edges, and sprinkle with the ginger or lemon rind. Roll up the pastry very carefully and seal the edges securely with a little milk or water, to prevent the syrup seeping out. Roll up in a clean, floured pudding cloth and tie the ends, but leaving room for the pudding to swell. Steam over a saucepan of boiling water for 1½ hours, topping up the water as necessary. Serve the pudding, cut into slices, accompanied by a warm syrup sauce, flavoured with a little ground ginger or lemon juice. Serves 4-6.

Hampshire Cod

2 lb. cod, cleaned and the head, tail and fins removed
3 oz. fresh white breadcrumbs
1½ oz. shredded suet
1 shallot or half a small onion, peeled and finely chopped
1 dessertspoon fresh, chopped parsley
1 teaspoon fresh, chopped thyme
Grated rind of a small lemon
Salt and black pepper
Pinch of ground nutmeg
1 egg, beaten
1-1½ oz. butter

Set oven to 350°F or Mark 4. Wipe the cod, inside and out with a piece of kitchen paper. Mix together the breadcrumbs, suet, shallot or onion, herbs, lemon rind, seasoning and nutmeg and bind with the beaten egg, to form a firm mixture. Use this to stuff the cod. Place the cod in a well greased ovenproof dish and dot with butter. Bake for 40-45 minutes, basting occasionally with any juices and covering with a piece of kitchen foil if the cod appears to be browning too quickly. Serve, cut into slices accompanied by boiled potatoes, peas and parsley or butter sauce. Serves 4-6.

If preferred a haddock can replace the cod, or the fish can be cut into thick cutlets and the stuffing spread on top of them for cooking.

Mothering Sunday Wafers

1½ oz. flour
1 teaspoon ground ginger
2 oz. golden syrup
1½ oz. caster sugar
2 oz. butter
1 to 2 teaspoons orange flower water

Set oven to 350°F or Mark 4. Sift together the flour and ground ginger. In a saucepan, melt together the syrup, sugar and butter, stirring until smooth. Remove from the heat, fold in the flour mixture, then stir in the orange flower water. Place teaspoonsful of the mixture on to buttered baking trays, allowing about 3 inches between them, to enable wafers to spread during cooking. Bake for 10 minutes, by which time the wafers will be golden-brown, thin and lace-like. Leave on the tray for 1 to 2 minutes then, using a palette knife, transfer to a wire rack. Serve spread with a jelly preserve (such as bramble jelly or similar), or with whipped cream. These wafers are usually served flat, but if desired can be wrapped round the buttered handle of a wooden spoon, to form a 'cigar' shape and filled later.

Bean and Bacon Soup

12 oz. dried haricot beans, soaked overnight in cold water
A little cooking oil
12 oz. streaky bacon, de-rinded and finely chopped
1 large onion, peeled and chopped
2½-3 pints chicken stock
2 sticks celery, washed, trimmed and finely chopped
1 medium carrot, peeled and finely sliced
1 bay leaf
Salt and black pepper
Pinch of ground cloves
1 lb. tomatoes, peeled and chopped
Chopped parsley to garnish

Drain the haricot beans and rinse well in cold water. Heat the cooking oil in a frying pan and fry the bacon until lightly browned. Remove with a slotted spoon and place in a large saucepan. Fry the onion until soft in the remaining oil, then add to the saucepan. Add the stock, celery, carrot, haricot beans, bay leaf, seasoning and spice. Bring to the boil, then cover and simmer for 1-1½ hours. Then stir in the tomatoes and simmer gently for a further 30-40 minutes until the haricot beans are very tender. Remove the bay leaf and serve the soup, garnished with chopped parsley and accompanied by granary bread. Serves 4-6.

If preferred tinned tomatoes can be substituted for the fresh ones.

Honey and Walnut Tartlets

6 oz. flour
Pinch of salt
8 oz. butter, softened
1 egg yolk
¼ pint soured cream
5 tablespoons clear honey
4 tablespoons soft brown sugar
4 oz. finely chopped walnuts
1 teaspoon lemon juice

Sift the flour and salt together into a bowl, then rub in the butter until the mixture resembles fine breadcrumbs. Add the egg yolk and the cream and knead lightly to form a smooth paste. Roll into a ball and chill for 1-1½ hours. Set oven to 375°F or Mark 5. Roll out the pastry on a lightly floured surface – handle it carefully as it is inclined to be 'short' – and use to line 12-14 greased and floured tartlet tins. Mix together the honey, sugar, walnuts and lemon juice and divide the mixture evenly between the tartlets. Bake for about 15-20 minutes until the pastry is lightly golden and the filling crisp.

Gypsy Bread

10 oz. self-raising flour
Pinch of salt
½ teaspoon mixed spice
½ teaspoon ground ginger
4 oz. soft brown sugar
4 oz. sultanas
2 oz. chopped mixed peel
6 oz. black treacle
1 tablespoon milk
1 egg, beaten
¼ teaspoon bicarbonate of soda
2 teaspoons milk

Set oven to 350°F or Mark 4. Sift the flour, salt and spices together into a bowl, then stir in the sugar, sultanas and mixed peel. Warm the treacle and milk together, then add the egg. Pour into the dry ingredients and whisk well together. Dissolve the bicarbonate of soda in the milk and add to the mixture, mixing well. Pour into a lightly greased 2 lb. loaf tin and bake for 40-45 minutes. Reduce the oven temperature to 325°F or Mark 3 and bake for a further 25-30 minutes, covering the top with kitchen foil if it browns too quickly. Cool in the tin for 10 minutes, then turn out on to a wire rack. Serve sliced, spread with butter.

Emery Down

Strawberries in Syrup

2 punnets of strawberries
2 oz. sugar
2 teaspoons brandy
¼ lb. redcurrant jelly
1 to 2 tablespoons of water
1 to 2 teaspoons of lemon juice
(if desired)

Hull the strawberries, rinse and drain well and cut into halves or quarters if large. Place in a bowl and sprinkle over the sugar and brandy. Cover and leave in a cool place overnight. Next day, melt the redcurrant jelly with the water and lemon juice (if desired) in a saucepan, then add the liquid from the strawberries. Heat through thoroughly. Add the strawberries and simmer gently for a few minutes, making sure that the fruit does not break up. Remove the strawberries with a slotted spoon and place in a serving dish. Bring the syrup to the boil, stirring. Allow to cool a little, then pour over the strawberries. Chill and serve decorated with a spray of maidenhair fern and accompanied by whipped cream. Serves 4 to 6.

Farmhouse Halibut

6 halibut steaks, wiped and the skin removed
Salt and black pepper
6 sprigs of parsley
½ to ¾ pint single cream
1½ to 2 oz. flour
1 tablespoon chopped fresh parsley
Parsley sprigs for garnish

Set oven to 325°F or Mark 3. Place the halibut steaks in a well buttered ovenproof dish. Season, then place a sprig of parsley on each steak. Pour the cream over, cover the dish with a lid or a piece of lightly-buttered foil and cook for 30 to 35 minutes. Remove the halibut steaks with a slotted spoon and place on a warm serving dish. Strain the cooking liquid. Reserving a little, place the remainder in a clean saucepan. Blend the flour with the reserved liquid until smooth, then add to the remainder of the liquid. Bring to the boil, stirring, until the sauce has thickened; adjust the seasoning if necessary, then stir in the chopped parsley and simmer, stirring, for 1 minute. Spoon the sauce over the fish and garnish with parsley sprigs. Serve with creamed potatoes, peas and carrots. Serves 6.

Mustard Rabbit

1 young rabbit, cleaned and jointed
2 oz. flour
Salt and black pepper
1 teaspoon dry mustard powder
A little cooking oil
½ lb. belly pork, skinned, boned and cubed
2 carrots, peeled and sliced
1 large onion, peeled and chopped
1 tablespoon fresh, chopped parsley
2 teaspoons fresh, chopped thyme
1 bay leaf
Salt and black pepper
½ pint dry cider
Chicken stock
3 egg yolks
A good ¼ pint double cream
1 level tablespoon dry mustard powder
Fresh, chopped parsley for garnish

Set oven to 350°F or Mark 4. Mix flour, seasoning, mustard and coat rabbit. Heat oil in a pan and lightly fry rabbit. Place half pork and half vegetables in a casserole and place rabbit joints on top. Add herbs and seasoning and top with remaining pork and vegetables. Pour cider into pan and boil. Pour into casserole with sufficient hot stock just to cover. Cover and cook for 1½ to 2 hours until tender. Remove meat and vegetables and place in warm serving dish. Strain liquid into pan and boil to reduce. Beat together egg yolks, cream and mustard, add 3 to 4 tablespoons of liquid and whisk. Pour into remainder of liquid and heat through thoroughly, but *do not* boil or sauce will curdle. Adjust seasoning, adding mustard if necessary, then spoon over rabbit. Serve, garnished with parsley, with creamed potatoes and green vegetable. Serves 4 to 6.

Seventeen

Lenten Pie

1 lb. prepared shortcrust pastry
1 oz. butter
1 onion, peeled and chopped
1 clove garlic, peeled and crushed
2 to 3 bunches of watercress, trimmed, rinsed, well-drained and chopped
3 eggs, beaten
¼ pint milk
¼ pint single cream
2 to 3 tablespoons fresh, chopped herbs parsley, chives, thyme etc.
Salt and black pepper
¼ teaspoon grated nutmeg
1 heaped tablespoon grated cheese (if desired)

If desired this can be served as a flan by halving the pastry requirement and omitting the pastry lid.

Set oven to 375°F or Mark 5. Grease a 9 inch flan dish. Roll out the pastry on a lightly floured surface and use half to line the flan dish, trimming the edges neatly. Bake blind for 15 to 20 minutes. Melt the butter in a saucepan and cook the onion and garlic until soft then add the watercress and cook for 1 to 2 minutes, stirring once or twice. Beat the eggs and milk together, then stir in the cream, herbs, seasoning and nutmeg. Add the watercress mixture and combine well. Turn into the flan dish and sprinkle over the grated cheese, if desired. Top with the remaining pastry, sealing the edges well and trimming neatly. Make a small steam hole in the centre and glaze with a little milk or beaten egg. Bake for about 30 minutes until the filling is set and the pastry top golden. Serve hot or cold. Serves 4 to 6.

Passford Farm

Hampshire Goose

8 lightly fried sausages or any left-over cold cooked ham or pork
4 large potatoes, peeled and sliced
2 onions, peeled and sliced
2 medium-sized cooking apples, peeled, cored and sliced
1 teaspoon chopped fresh sage
Salt and black pepper
½ pint pork stock
A small 'walnut' of butter
4 oz. Cheddar cheese, grated

Set oven to 350°F or Mark 4. Place a layer of potato in the base of a lightly greased casserole dish, cover with a layer of onion, followed by a layer of apple and sprinkle with a little sage and season. Continue layering in this way until *half* the vegetables, apple and sage have been used up. Place the sausages, or cold cooked ham or pork which has been sliced, on top. Layer as before, finishing with potatoes. Pour in the stock and dot the top of the 'Goose' with the butter. Cook for 45-50 minutes, covering with a piece of kitchen foil if the top appears to be browning too quickly. Remove from the oven and sprinkle on the grated cheese. Return to the oven and cook for a further 5-6 minutes until the cheese is golden and bubbling. Serves 4.

Picnic Cake

4 oz. butter
8 oz. sugar
3 eggs, beaten together
6 oz. flour
½ teaspoon baking powder
¼ teaspoon salt
½ teaspoon ground nutmeg
¼ teaspoon ground cinnamon
2 tablespoons milk
¼ teaspoon bicarbonate of soda
2 tablespoons clear honey
6 oz. walnut kernels – 6 reserved for decoration, the rest roughly chopped
6 oz. raisins or sultanas

Set oven to 325°F or Mark 3. Cream the butter and sugar together in a bowl until light and fluffy, and beat in a little of the eggs. Sift the flour, baking powder, salt and spices together, then add alternately to the creamed mixture with the remainder of the eggs. Warm the milk slightly and stir in the honey, then add the bicarbonate of soda and stir into the mixture. Add the chopped nuts and dried fruit and combine well together. Spoon the mixture into a well greased and lightly floured 2 lb. loaf tin and bake for 1-1½ hours, covering the top with kitchen foil if it appears to be browning too quickly. Place the reserved walnuts on the top of the cake, and bake for a further 40-45 minutes. Cool in the tin for 30 minutes, then turn out on to a wire rack.

Watercress Flan

8 oz. shortcrust pastry
1 onion, peeled and finely sliced
2 oz. butter
2 bunches watercress trimmed and chopped
Salt and black pepper
A few drops Worcestershire sauce
2 eggs
¼ pint milk
5 fl. oz. single cream
Watercress sprigs for garnish

Set oven to 400°F or Mark 6. Roll out the pastry on a lightly floured surface and use to line a lightly greased 8 inch flan dish. Bake blind for 10 minutes. Fry the onions in the butter until soft, but not coloured, then stir in the watercress. Cook, stirring lightly, for 3 minutes. Add the seasoning and Worcestershire sauce and transfer the mixture to the flan case, spreading out evenly. Beat the eggs, milk and cream lightly together and pour over the mixture. Reduce oven temperature to 375°F or Mark 5 and bake the flan for 25-30 minutes or until set and golden. Serve hot or cold, garnished with the reserved watercress sprigs. Serves 4-6.

New Forest Venison

2 lb. venison, minced
8 oz. fat bacon, de-rinded and minced
1 onion, peeled and finely chopped
6 oz. fresh white breadcrumbs
1 tablespoon fresh, chopped parsley
Grated rind of half a lemon
Salt and black pepper
2 eggs, beaten
Beef stock
Parsley sprigs for garnish

In a bowl mix together the venison, bacon, onion, breadcrumbs, parsley, lemon rind and seasoning and stir in the beaten egg. Bind the mixture with a little stock. Flour a clean pudding cloth, place the mixture on it and form into a thick roll. Roll up firmly and tie the ends. Wrap the roll in kitchen foil to form a parcel. Place in a saucepan of boiling water and boil for 2-2½ hours, topping up the water if necessary. Serve, cut into thick slices, garnished with parsley and accompanied by creamed potatoes, a green vegetable, a rich brown gravy and cranberry jelly. Serves 4-6.

This dish is traditionally cooked by boiling, but, if preferred the mixture can be cooked in a large, well greased pudding basin in a saucepan of boiling water for 2½-2¾ hours.

Furzey Lodge, near Beaulieu

Bachelor's Pudding

2 or 3 cooking apples, peeled, cored and chopped to provide 4 oz. of apple flesh
4 oz. fresh white breadcrumbs
4 oz. currants or sultanas
3 oz. caster sugar
Grated rind of half a lemon
Pinch grated nutmeg
Pinch salt
1 dessertspoon melted butter
2 small eggs, beaten
A little milk
½ teaspoon baking powder

Butter a 2 pint pudding basin. In a bowl, mix together the apples, breadcrumbs, dried fruit and sugar and then stir in the lemon rind, nutmeg and salt. Add the melted butter and beaten eggs, stir well, cover and leave to stand in a cool place for 20 to 30 minutes. Then mix in sufficient milk to give a dropping consistency and stir in the baking powder. Spoon into the pudding basin and smooth over. Cover with buttered greaseproof paper and kitchen foil and tie down. Place in a steamer set over a saucepan of boiling water and steam for 2½ to 3 hours, topping up the water as necessary. Turn out on to a warm serving plate and serve with custard. Serves 4-6.

Lardy Cake

½ teaspoon sugar
3 fl oz. warm milk
1 teaspoon dried yeast
¾ lb. strong white flour
¼ oz. salt
¼ oz. lard or margarine
4 oz. lard
4 oz. granulated sugar
A good half teaspoon each of ground nutmeg, cinnamon and allspice
1 oz. granulated sugar
2 tablespoons milk

Dissolve the sugar in the milk, then sprinkle on the yeast and leave in a warm place until it is dissolved and frothy – about 10 minutes. Mix the flour and salt together in a bowl and rub in the ¼ oz. fat. Make a well in the centre and stir in the yeast mixture to form a firm, but not sticky dough. Turn out on to a lightly floured surface and knead until the dough is smooth – about 10 minutes. Form into a ball, place in a clean bowl, cover with a clean teacloth and leave to rise in a warm place until it has doubled in bulk. Then knock back and knead again on a lightly floured surface until the dough is firm – about 2 minutes – then roll out into a rectangle, about 10 inches by 6 inches. Cut the lard into flakes and dot one third of the flakes over two thirds of the dough, then sprinkle over one third of the sugar. Fold up the uncovered third part of the dough and then fold the top third down to form a 'parcel', sealing the ends with a rolling pin. Give a half turn to the dough and roll out again; add the lard and sugar as before and sprinkle over half of the spices. Repeat the folding process once more. Then roll the dough out again and fold without any additions. Finally roll out to fit a 7 inch square cake tin that has been well greased with lard. Cover with a clean tea cloth and leave to prove in a warm place for 30 minutes. Set oven to 450°F or Mark 8. Score the top of the lardy cake in squares and bake for 25 to 30 minutes. Dissolve the 1 oz. sugar in the milk and boil in a pan until syrupy to form a glaze. Brush this over the hot lardy cake in the tin and leave for 2 minutes. Remove the lardy cake from the tin, put upside down on a wire rack over a plate to drain and spoon any lard or syrup left in the tin over the base of the cake. Serve upside down, broken into pieces (for Hampshire Lardy Cake should never be cut) with or without butter.

Originally this yeast cake was made with dough left over from a bread-making session. There are numerous county lardy cake recipes in existence, but it is said that a true Hampshire Lardy Cake contains no fruit and is always turned upside down to drain after cooking.

Buttered Trout

6 trout, cleaned and gutted
Sea salt
1½ oz. flour
Salt and black pepper
A pinch of dry mustard
A pinch of nutmeg
3 oz. butter
The juice of a lemon
Lemon slices and parsley sprigs for garnish

Sprinkle the trout, inside and out, with sea salt and leave in a cool place for about an hour. Wipe the trout well, inside and out, with a piece of damp kitchen paper. Mix together the flour, seasoning, mustard and nutmeg and use to coat the trout. Melt the butter in a frying pan and fry the trout, allowing about 3 to 5 minutes on each side. Remove the trout with a slotted spoon and place on a warm serving dish. Stir the lemon juice into the remaining butter in the frying pan, heat through and pour over the trout. Serve at once, garnished with lemon slices and parsley sprigs, and accompanied by boiled or new potatoes. Serves 6.

The Test near Romsey

Pork with Nuts

3½ to 4 lb. pork joint – top leg is ideal
1oz. flour
Salt and black pepper
Pinch of dried sage
3 oz. shelled walnuts, finely chopped
2 oz. shelled hazelnuts or blanched almonds, finely chopped
3 oz. fresh brown breadcrumbs
Salt
1 oz. butter

Set oven to 400°F or Mark 6. Mix the flour with the seasoning and dried sage and rub all over the pork joint. Mix the nuts with the breadcrumbs and season with a little salt. Butter a large roasting tin, particularly down the centre and spoon the nut mixture on to this, patting it into a loose, flattish cake. Set the pork on a roasting rack in the tin and over the nut mixture and roast for 2½ hours, basting the pork from time to time. Transfer to a heated serving dish, remove the nut mixture with a slotted spoon and sprinkle over the joint, pressing down on the top. Serve with roast potatoes, baked onions and a green vegetable and accompanied by redcurrant jelly. Serves 4 to 6.

Devilled Chicken

8 chicken legs, cooked
2 teaspoons English mustard powder
½ teaspoon salt
½ teaspoon black pepper
½ teaspoon cayenne pepper
½ teaspoon paprika
2 teaspoons curry powder
2 teaspoons French mustard
2 oz. butter, softened
1 tablespoon flour
Slices of hot buttered toast
Parsley sprigs for garnish

The chicken legs should first be baked, with the skin on, until cooked but not browned and then allowed to get cold. Mix the mustard powder together with *half* of each of the salt, black pepper, cayenne pepper and paprika. Stir in the curry powder and French mustard to form a paste. Add *half* the butter and blend together until the mixture is smooth. Make 3-4 slits in each chicken leg, and spread the 'devil' mixture into each. Mix the flour together with the remaining salt, black pepper, cayenne pepper and paprika and dust over the chicken legs. Melt the remaining butter and lightly brush over the chicken legs. Place the chicken legs under a hot grill for 5 minutes, turning to brown them on all sides, and basting with any juices that form in the pan. Serve at once, garnished with parsley sprigs and accompanied by hot buttered toast, cut into fingers.

Cucumber and Stilton Mousse

1 pint aspic jelly, made up according to the packet instructions
8 oz. Stilton cheese (rind removed) finely crumbled
The juice of half a lemon
A pinch of white pepper
8 oz. cucumber, peeled and very finely chopped
½ pint whipping cream
Sliced cucumber and chopped parsley for garnish

Allow the aspic to cool until it is on the point of setting, then put in a liquidiser with the cheese, lemon juice and pepper and blend until smooth – similar to thin cream. Pour into a mixing bowl and stir in the chopped cucumber. Whip the cream until it just holds its shape and fold into the mixture. Rinse a 2 pint ring mould with very cold water and pour in the mixture. Place in the refrigerator and chill until set – ideally overnight. Turn out on to a serving plate – if it appears to stick, dip the mould *very* quickly into hot water – and garnish with the cucumber slices, overlapped around the top of the mousse and sprinkled with parsley. Serve with triangles of buttered brown bread. Serves 4-6.

Hampshire Haslet

2 lb. lean pork, coarsely minced
8 oz. stale white bread, cubed
Milk or water for soaking
1 medium onion, peeled and chopped
1 teaspoon fresh chopped sage
Salt and black pepper

Soak the bread in sufficient milk or water to cover and, when soft, squeeze out the excess moisture. Set the oven to 375°F or Mark 5. Mix together the bread, pork, onion, sage and seasoning. Put through a fine mincer. Lightly grease a 2½-3 lb. loaf tin. Put the mixture into the tin and press down firmly and evenly. Bake for 1½-2 hours, covering the top with kitchen foil if it browns too quickly. Allow to cool slightly in the tin, then turn out and allow to cool completely. Serve cold, sliced, with salad and boiled potatoes. Serves 4-6

Haslet comes from the Old French word for entrails but basically refers to the fact that all the ingredients are very finely minced.

Buckler's Hard

Cornflour Cake

4 oz. butter, softened
8 oz. sugar
5 oz. cornflour
9 oz. flour
1 teaspoon baking powder
Pinch of salt
4 eggs, separated
A few drops of vanilla or almond essence
Icing sugar for topping

Set oven to 375°F or Mark 5. Cream the butter and *half* the sugar together in a bowl until very light and fluffy. Sift together the cornflour, flour, baking powder and salt. Beat the egg yolks with the remaining 4 ozs sugar until creamy, add to the butter mixture and beat thoroughly, then stir in the vanilla or almond essence. Fold in the dry ingredients. Then whisk the egg whites until they stand up into soft peaks and fold into the mixture. Turn into a greased and lightly floured 8 inch round cake tin and bake for 1 to 1¼ hours, covering the top with a piece of kitchen foil if it appears to be browning too quickly. Test with a skewer to see when done. Cool in the tin for 5 minutes, then turn out on to a wire rack. Dust the top with a little sifted icing sugar before serving.

Poacher's Pie

2½ to 3 lb. mixed game – rabbit, venison, pheasant etc. – cubed and dusted with seasoned flour
1 medium onion, peeled and sliced
A little cooking oil
4 oz. mushrooms, wiped and sliced
½ teaspoon ground nutmeg
4 oz. chestnuts, cooked and peeled
2 teaspoons fresh, chopped parsley
Grated rind of half a lemon
Salt and black pepper
½ pint pork stock
1 tablespoon red wine or port – optional
8 oz. shortcrust pastry
Beaten egg to glaze

Set oven to 400°F or Mark 6. Fry the onion in the oil until soft, but not brown, then mix with the game, mushrooms, chestnuts, parsley, nutmeg, lemon rind and seasoning. Place in a deep 2-3 pint pie dish, inserting a pie funnel if necessary. Mix the stock with the wine or port, if used, and pour just over half over the pie filling. Roll out the pastry on a lightly floured surface, line the rim of dish with a dampened strip and then cover the pie, sealing the edges well. Trim and flute. Make a steam hole and use trimmings to decorate. Brush with beaten egg and bake for 1-1½ hours, reducing temperature to 350°F or Mark 4 after 30 minutes, covering with kitchen foil if it browns too quickly. When cooked, heat the remaining stock and top up the pie if necessary. Serve with boiled potatoes, carrots and a green vegetable. Serves 4-6.

Hampshire Herrings

6 herrings, cleaned, gutted and with heads, tails and fins removed
1 large onion, peeled and finely chopped
6 to 8 peppercorns
6 to 8 sprigs of parsley
2 to 3 small strips of lemon rind
1 bay leaf
¼ pint white wine vinegar
¼ pint port wine
¼ pint water
Lemon slices and parsley sprigs for garnish

Set oven to 350°F or Mark 4. Lightly butter an ovenproof dish and place the herrings in it, close together side-by-side and head to tail. Sprinkle over the onion, peppercorns, parsley and lemon rind and place the bay leaf on top. Mix together the vinegar, port wine and water and pour over. Place in the oven and cook for 40 to 45 minutes. If they are to be served hot, remove the fish from the liquid and serve garnished with lemon slices and parsley sprigs. If to be served cold, allow to cool in the liquid. Serve the hot Hampshire Herrings with boiled potatoes and crusty bread and the cold ones with potato salad and crusty bread. Serves 6.

Hampshire Syllabub

¼ pint strong beer
4 oz. caster sugar
½ teaspoon grated nutmeg
2 to 3 tablespoons brandy
1 pint double cream

Put the beer into a bowl and stir in the sugar and nutmeg; then stir in the brandy and leave to infuse for 1 to 2 hours. Chill the cream well and pour into a bowl. Add the beer mixture and whisk until very thick. Spoon into deep glasses and chill for several hours – this will bring out the flavour. Serve with cat's tongue biscuits. Serves 6 to 8.

Traditionally, syllabubs are served without decoration but, if desired, this one can be topped with a few raisins or sultanas that have been soaked in a little brandy.

Palace House, Beaulieu

Hampshire Drops

4 oz. butter or margarine
4 oz. sugar
1 egg, beaten
4 oz. self-raising flour
4 oz. cornflour
Pinch of salt
Jam – preferably raspberry
Sifted icing sugar

Set oven to 375°F or Mark 5. In a bowl, cream the butter or margarine together with the sugar until very light and fluffy and beat in a little of the egg. Sift the flour, cornflour and salt together, then add alternately with the remainder of the egg to the creamed mixture, beating well between each addition. Fold in any remaining flour. Place heaped teaspoons of the mixture on to lightly greased baking sheets, allowing room for spreading, and bake for about 10 minutes until golden. Cool on a wire rack, then sandwich the drops together with jam and dust the tops lightly with sifted icing sugar.

Venison Pasty

2 lb. venison, wiped and cut into small steaks
2 oz. flour
Salt and black pepper
2 oz. butter
¼ pint stock
The juice of half a lemon
¼ pint port wine
2 teaspoons ground nutmeg
1 heaped dessertspoon fresh chopped herbs – parsley, chives, thyme etc.
2 to 3 oz. lamb suet (if desired)
¾ to 1 lb. prepared puff pastry (shortcrust can be used if preferred)
Beaten egg to glaze

Because venison is a somewhat dry meat the lamb suet was included to add moisture, but it can be omitted.

Set oven to 425°F or Mark 7. Mix the flour and seasoning and coat the venison. Melt the butter in a pan and brown the meat on all sides. Transfer to a 2 to 3 pint deep pie dish. Pour the stock into the pan and bring to the boil, stirring. Pour over the meat and allow to cool a little. Add the lemon juice, port wine, nutmeg and herbs, then lay over the suet, if desired. Roll out the pastry on a lightly floured surface, line the rim of the dish with a dampened strip and then cover the pie, sealing the edges well. Trim and flute. Make a steam hole and use trimmings to decorate. Brush with beaten egg and bake for 1½ to 2 hours, reducing the temperature to 350°F or Mark 4 after 15 minutes, covering with kitchen foil if it browns too quickly. Serve with creamed potatoes, baked onions and a green vegetable. Serves 4 to 6.

Hampshire Roll

4 oz. sugar
4 oz. butter, softened
2 eggs, beaten
4 oz. flour
Pinch of salt
Grated rind of half a lemon
3 cooking apples, peeled, cored and sliced
3 tablespoons apricot jam
A little sifted icing sugar

Set oven to 350°F or Mark 4. In a bowl cream the sugar and butter together until light and fluffy, then stir in the eggs, a little at a time. Sift the flour and salt together and fold into the mixture, then stir in the lemon rind. Spoon half the mixture into a well buttered 2 pint pie dish and smooth over. Arrange the apple slices on top and spread with the apricot jam. Cover with the remaining mixture and smooth over. Bake for 30-40 minutes until golden brown. Serve hot, dusted with icing sugar and accompanied by cream, custard or apricot jam sauce. Serves 4.

This is not really a roll at all, but a layered pudding.

METRIC CONVERSIONS

The weights, measures and oven temperatures used in the preceding recipes can be easily converted to their metric equivalents.

Weights

Avoirdupois	**Metric**
1 oz.	just under 30 grams
4 oz. (¼ lb.)	app. 115 grams
8 oz. (½ lb.)	app. 230 grams
1 lb.	454 grams

Liquid Measures

Imperial	**Metric**
1 tablespoon (liquid only)	20 millilitres
1 fl. oz.	app. 30 millilitres
1 gill (¼ pt.)	app. 145 millilitres
½ pt.	app. 285 millilitres
1 pt.	app. 570 millilitres
1 qt.	app. 1.140 litres

Oven Temperatures

	°Fahrenheit	Gas Mark	°Celsius
Slow	300	2	140
	325	3	158
Moderate	350	4	177
	375	5	190
	400	6	204
Hot	425	7	214
	450	8	232
	500	9	260

Flour as specified in these recipes refers to Plain Flour unless otherwise described.